DIANA
PRINCESS OF WALES

Trevor Hall

Designed by Philip Clucas MSIAD

Produced by Ted Smart and David Gibbon

GREENWICH HOUSE

Just what is it about her? More than two years under the incessant gaze of the public eye have left Diana, Princess of Wales less of an enigma than she was, but her popularity, seemingly boundless as it increases almost by the week, has every social commentator, every royal-watcher, and even her own admirers stumped for adequate or logical explanations. Those unseen authorities at Buckingham Palace, no less, have been openly confounded by successive waves of interest which have threatened to put her in danger of constant Press harrassment: as early as December 1981 the royal spokesmen were protesting their genuine and mildly horrified concern that the Royal Wedding

Facing page: *A shy Lady Diana coped admirably with the unwanted attentions of a Press bent on verifying rumours of a royal engagement. The official announcement of the betrothal, made on 24th February 1981* top left, *must have come as a welcome relief from the enforced secrecy of the previous months.* Right and far right: *A relaxed Lady Diana attends her first official function, a music recital at London's Goldsmiths Hall, where she met the late Princess Grace of Monaco.*

had failed to have its expected cathartic effect, and that Diana was no nearer being able to enjoy a modicum of privacy than she had been before.

That particular official disclosure followed one of the many incidents in which Diana's position – possibly naively unsought but certainly inescapable – in the centre of the national and even international social stage led to worrying excesses of journalistic zeal. Like all of Prince Charles' many girlfriends, real or imagined, Diana was quickly spotted as the stuff (to paraphrase the Archbishop of Canterbury) of which good press stories and profitable newspaper sales are made. So it was a natural consequence that, during what must have seemed an interminable courtship, she was hounded so relentlessly by the world's Press that eventually her mother felt constrained to

Official portraits and photographs of Lady Diana's every outing were eagerly awaited by a public that had taken her to its heart. Wherever she appeared eager crowds gathered to admire and cheer a future queen who had undertaken her duties with the goodnatured professionalism of

one born to the job. Above and facing page right: *The Prince and Lady Diana visit Tetbury, just a few miles from Highgrove, their future home.* Facing page left: *Lady Diana at Ascot and* bottom centre *at the wedding of Christopher Soames and Catherine Weatherall.*

drop a few diplomatic paragraphs of complaint on her behalf to The Times. And that, after her engagement, comments upon that famous black evening dress, which she wore for the first and last time in public, were almost universally

Right and facing page: *Two official portraits of a princess-to-be.* Below: *Lady Diana steals the limelight from the Prince of Wales at her first official function. At Royal Ascot* bottom centre *and Broadlands* right, *home of the late Lord Mountbatten.* Above: *During the Trooping the Colour ceremony.*

confined to its daringly low neckline. Some observers even thought it revealed more than it was intended to – an allegation which others put down to wishful thinking or a trick of the light. Only a few days before her wedding she found herself again the unwilling target of Press attention at polo matches as, it seemed, every photographer in the world virtually chased her round spectators' enclosures at Windsor and Tidworth: at the

Royal Ascot week has been an important date in the social life of British royalty since the event was instituted by Queen Anne in 1711. Nominally a four-day race meeting held each June, it is essentially a social and fashion event that focuses greater attention on the headwear of the ladies than performance of the horses. Prominent members of the Royal Family are invariably present throughout the four days, and in 1981 it was Lady Diana, accompanied by a variety of escorts, who proved to be the main attraction. Overleaf: The splendour of the wedding day.

latter she eventually broke down and had to be led away in tears. No fewer than seventy photographers travelled hot-foot to Balmoral the following month just for a few pictures of her with Prince Charles on their return from honeymoon in the Mediterranean. That December, another posse of photographers snooped from behind the bushes at Highgrove to catch Diana hugging Charles on the doorstep of their country home. Two months later two newspapers sent photographers to Eleuthera, where they took pictures of Diana, now showing visible signs of pregnancy, sunbathing in a bikini, and in doing so attracted the publicly-voiced concern of the Queen for

Television pictures of the day's happy events were beamed to record audiences throughout the world, whilst a crowd estimated at 650,000 lined London's streets to cheer the couple.

having invaded her daughter-in-law's privacy. Throughout her pregnancy, however, Diana's privacy has always remained at risk as public interest has, understandably, shown no sign of waning.

Given that, however unpardonable their methods, the media merely reflect the public interest (or, more accurately, help to create that interest which the public is more

With public jubilation still in progress, the Prince and Princess of Wales left Buckingham Palace for Waterloo station in a suitably decorated horse-drawn carriage top *to begin their honeymoon. Two days of relaxation at Broadlands were followed by a flight to Gibraltar* above and right, *where the couple joined the Royal Yacht Britannia for a Mediterranean cruise, facing page.*

than willing to take up), why has it all happened so spontaneously to this one very young woman? Why was 1981, with more than its fair share of national and international tragedy and danger, dubbed 'The Year of The Princess'? Why have two major American TV companies spent millions competing to produce the less dreadful narrative account of her last thirty months? Why have more column-inches been written in newspapers, magazines and books, more words been spoken on television and radio, more

feet of film, still or movie, been expended on account of this most famous of instant celebrities than on any other in living memory? What quirk of the personality cult has put her name on everyone's lips as readily as any film star's, when she has won no Oscars? Or made her features as instantly recognisable as any world leader's, when she has gained no diplomatic battles? Or made her reputation as prominent as the most successful sportsman, when she has scored no goals and won no medals?

On their return from the honeymoon, Charles and Diana joined the rest of the Royal Family on their summer break at Balmoral. These pages: The newlyweds pose for Press photographers in Scotland.

Even a personal interview – a privilege she has yet to grant – would probably not answer these questions satisfactorily, though one can point to all sorts of things that might help. Is it primarily her youth – that fresh, bright sparkle which, even at the side of her own fiancé, seems to be rejuvenating the institution of monarchy at a stroke, with the vitality of a vigorous young lady

on the verge of accomplishing maturity? At nineteen, as she was then, she appeared to be the catalyst for the emergence of that bevy of royal teenagers who have been content to wait in the wings until quite recently. Her wedding day appearance on the palace balcony, surrounded by so many children, was a symbol of that regeneration. Flanked by a family of in-laws creeping towards increasing staidness, with the Queen herself almost as revered as any of her august matriarchal ancestresses, Diana received the sort of ecstatic acclaim once reserved for Elizabeth II herself in the earliest years of her reign.

In October 1981, with the holiday finally over, Diana began her official round of duties as the Princess of Wales with, appropriately enough, a three-day tour of the Principality. Despite the rather inclement weather and a number of anti-royalist and nationalist protests, the Princess appeared to enjoy meeting the Welsh people who had turned out to greet her, and the tour proved a resounding success.

That is not to suggest that the Queen is about to be permanently upstaged, or that Diana could teach her a thing or two about creating a rapport with her people. The Queen's more restrictive role, and her deeply inculcated empathy toward the inherited dignity of her position make it difficult to avoid distancing herself circumspectly from all but relatively few of her subjects, or to get involved physically or conversationally in anything which might suggest the remotest taint of gimmickry or the second-rate. Any loss of face would be a disaster she would not care to court. Diana, on the other hand, has enjoyed relative

Since the earliest announcement of Diana's engagement to the Prince of Wales, her general appearance and dress sense have been the subject of close assessment, continuous discussion and not infrequent emulation. Even the cut of her hair inspired coiffeurs to offer women the new "Di look." Wherever she appears note is made of the colour and style of her clothes and it is a compliment to her taste, that copies of some of the more notable designs subsequently appear in shop windows. Above and facing page: The Princess sported a fashionable high ruff and dashing feathered hat by Bellville-Sassoon on the third day of her Welsh visit.

The now famous, and unexpectedly low-cut, evening gown that Lady Diana wore on the occasion of her début, facing page bottom left, made it clear that in the matter of clothes, she would set, rather than follow, design trends.

freedom, unaffected by the limitations of the very highest protocol. Both as fiancée and wife of the Prince of Wales, she has been able to set her own pace, adopt her own guidelines and pursue her own natural and unaffected way with the people who will one day be her husband's subjects. In doing so she has shown that there is a place for youth in a revered institution, and she may already have prevented the onset of a crustiness which has often been criticised in long-established and unchanging courts of previous eras.

Few would rate Britain's latest Princess as ravishingly beautiful – her profile betrays a hint of what in an earlier age would have been called plainness – but she sports a vivacious

From shy and retiring kindergarten teacher to public and outgoing Princess; Diana's change of roles in the few months of her short engagement was nothing if not remarkable.

attractiveness which has made her something of a heroine in the eyes of even the most hard-bitten sceptics. It comprises all those qualities which traditionally capture the imagination of the male sex, and provoke the envy of her own. Those large eyes and generous mouth combine a tantalising sensuality with the modesty of the downward glance and the resolute secrecy of the tight-lipped reaction. The equally generous sweep of her hair has remained essentially simple, unsophisticated even on her wedding day, when no artificiality was required to accommodate her first tiara: yet that famous style has become the subject of imitation throughout the Western World, where Diana lookalikes enjoy a status symbol all their own. It has certainly been enough to give her regular hair-stylist, Kevin Shanley, confidence in his treatment of his client of four

A radiant Princess of Wales, her bouts of morning sickness now happily over, visited Guildford Cathedral with her husband in December 1981. On this their last public engagement before the Christmas and New Year break at Sandringham and Windsor, the couple attended a carol service in aid of the Prince's Trust for disadvantaged children, watched the performance of a nativity play and took part in the cutting of a Christmas cake.

years' standing. When, in April 1982, an American fashion expert, so called, condemned Diana's hair-style as out-of-date, Shanley merely said: 'The guy doesn't know what he's talking about,' and went on coiffing as before.

As for her clothes, the Emanuels made Diana with those superbly voluminous evening gowns, and Belleville-Sassoon capped it all with an unending succession of hats with their swashbuckling ostrich-feather trimmings in beige, aubergine, cantaloupe – soft feminine shades in a season when others paraded vibrant primary colours and harshly

Pregnancy, as well as a number of public appearances, began to take their toll on Diana's health towards the end of March and it was on the advice of her doctors that the Prince and Princess decided to take a 4-day break on St Mary's, largest of the Scilly Isles, where the Prince has a holiday home.

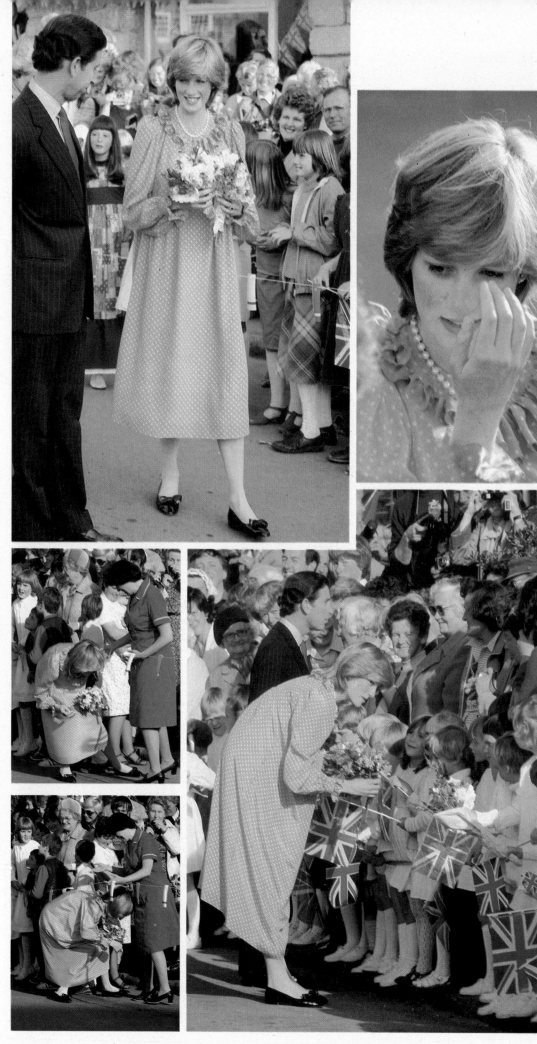

gleaming headgear. In her months of pregnancy the simple predominated – heavy, sometimes rugged coats during the winter months, and expansive, floaty maternity smocks worn time and again during the spring and summer, with the odd light coat or cardigan thrown over the shoulders for protection against

cool breezes. There were few
concessions to the great
occasion, though evening
dresses brought out the best in
her – velvet, silk taffeta, chiffon
all enhanced her femininity
without emphasising her

*The Prince and Princess arrived at
St Mary's to a warm reception* right
and facing page left. *They spent
the following day visiting the island
of Tresco which they reached by
private boat* above and facing
page right.

condition. She has, naturally enough, suffered the occasional fashion disaster: the fussy, limp dress with the top-heavy hat she sported for the 1981 Trooping, and the shapeless, oppressive, slightly shaggy coat and dated hat she wore at Huddersfield, Cheltenham and Aintree in February and March 1982. But her successes have been more noticeable. Her below-the-knee dresses and skirts have defied the influence of the mini-skirt's second coming: no tall girl in the whole country could fail to applaud her for popularising the low-heeled or flat shoe: and she did for the frilly ruff and the small choker what Queen Victoria did for the flounced cap, Queen Mary for the toque and Queen Elizabeth II for the headscarf.

No impression of Diana surpasses that of being the Princess who broke just about every rule in the book. That first low-cut evening dress was as much a declaration of independence as anything – no regulation or standard gown for her – and it was followed by a

whole chapter of behavioural novelties which, mistakenly, no-one imagined would last if she were to become a fully integrated member of Britain's First Family. On walkabouts – a term she has interpreted much more liberally than most – she has dived into crowds, shaking hands with whoever put theirs her way. She has chatted, as few royals do, with all and sundry – not simply to the chosen few – and on all subjects. When it was known that her baby was on the way, few occasions went by without her making some reference to one or other aspect of motherhood, such as morning

For Diana, universal popularity meant a busy schedule in the latter part of 1981. Facing page and below: *First solo engagement, the switching-on of the Christmas lights in Regent St.* Bottom left: *Arriving for a soiree at the Royal Academy of Arts.* Centre left: *At the Victoria and Albert Museum for the "Splendours of the Gonzaga" exhibition.* Top left: *Returning to London from a visit to Huddersfield.*

36

sickness ('Nobody told me it would be like this,' she said in November 1981) or the sex or expected date of birth of her own child. With children she has been a sensational success: no proffered flower has been spurned, no request for a kiss unrequited. Who among her in-laws has crouched down to speak to children at and on their own level, carried babies around with her, stopped her car deliberately to accept posies from children who have strayed from the main crowd? Here is

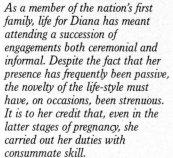

As a member of the nation's first family, life for Diana has meant attending a succession of engagements both ceremonial and informal. Despite the fact that her presence has frequently been passive, the novelty of the life-style must have, on occasions, been strenuous. It is to her credit that, even in the latter stages of pregnancy, she carried out her duties with consummate skill.

the same innovative approach which, sixty years before, marked out the lady who is now the Queen Mother as the genial

Both the Prince and Princess take an active interest in the life of the country's youth through involvement in various trusts and charities. Her evident love for and understanding of children make her a particularly popular figure amongst the young. This page: Diana attends a fund raising fair at a South London school in January 1982.

and persuasive debunker of outdated royal taboos within an institution fast becoming fossilised by the repressive deposits of Victorian protocol. Like her, Diana has not embarked on a specific crusade to ring the changes. Her approach is entirely natural, born of a fundamental fondness for others which her own past may have taught her was the only grace worth striving for,

both to acquire and to retain. So there is really no question of the Queen disapproving of her behaviour, as some commentators have alleged, any more than of persuading her to adopt, lock stock and barrel, all the favoured pursuits and life-style of generations of the Royal Family. She is inwardly convinced of what she finds

The Royal Family are regular visitors to the Highland Games at Braemar. Diana's elegant plaid dress facing page was the perfect choice for the occasion. Top right: Loyal Merseysiders turned out en masse to welcome the Princess on her visit to Liverpool. Above: Protective glasses and a baseball-style hat at the opening of a new electronics factory at Bridgend. Right: The Princess, sporting an attractive hat, meets interested youngsters during her tour of Deeside. Diana seems to share the predilection of other female members of the Royal Family for stylish headgear.

acceptable, and they take her or leave her as she is.

There is in this line of thought a stubborn streak in Diana, and some observers have not been slow to spot it and build on it. No-one seems quite sure whether it is a virtue or a fault – perhaps it depends upon who is the victim in each case. Her attitude to the Press has softened considerably in the last six months, but it was not so long ago that her glare of disapproval was every bit as imperious and withering as that

No truer word could have been spoken than when the Prince remarked on the 'wonderful effect' Diana seemed to have had on everyone and the announcement of her pregnancy, made on the morning of her visit to the Guildhall above, reinforced this.

of any queen-empress. There was no shortage of examples of her early influence over Prince Charles: his steeplechasing stopped, his valet was sacked, some long-term friends have, by all accounts, been cold-shouldered, his skiing and

fishing holidays have come to an end. While some of these changes might merely be the result of a variation in life-style common to all newly married men, the thread of steel running through Diana's willowy, feminine frame was all but visible as she dismissed two personal bodyguards in succession, picked a brief but well publicised quarrel with her husband while hunting at Sandringham, and showed persistent displeasure at a race meeting. Within days those columnists who were not busy foretelling the break-up of her marriage occupied themselves

The presence of royalty at any first night is guaranteed to awaken public interest and awareness in an event, and Diana's participation at such functions invariably has the desired effect.

building around these successive demonstrations of momentary dissatisfaction some intricately-worked and unattributed insights into Diana's long-term ambition, nourished from the age of fifteen, it was said, to become the wife of the heir to

Unlike the rest of the Royal Family, the Princess of Wales does not ride horses. Since her wedding however, Diana has begun to share in Prince Charles' interest in matters equestrian and, while she learns the finer points of horsemanship, there are always plenty of friends around to help in her education. The couple's visit to Liverpool in April coincided with the running of the Grand National at Aintree this page. The Princess evidently found the spectacle absorbing, watching part of this famous steeplechase from the bonnet of a Land Rover.

the Throne by hook or by crook. Even at that tender age she was, they alleged, watching Charles' courtship of her sister Sarah, looking for clues that would help her when her own turn came to attract his attentions and just waiting for her to make the fatal mistakes – which, of course, as in all fairy stories which end happily, she did. It was all riveting stuff. Popularity does not lend itself to easy analysis, but there can be little doubt that Diana's, much as it derives from her own personality, owes something to the fact that she is married to a very popular Prince. As the

twenty-first Prince of Wales,
Charles has quietly and
comprehensively outshone the
legendary reputations of two of
the most dazzling of his
predecessors, Edward VII and

*Like any other national institution,
the Royal Family have their fair
share of detractors who claim that
they serve no useful purpose. The
expressions on the faces of the public
wherever royalty appear are answer
enough. Prince Charles' engagement
and subsequent marriage did much
to re-awaken interest in the Royal
Family both in Britain and abroad,
with Diana high in the rankings as
one of its favourite members.*

Edward VIII, by the simple expedient of hard work, sympathetic concern, a thirst for fresh knowledge and experience, and an infectious sense of humour. The fact that, while he was single, every young girl and her mother yearned to kiss him (and many succeeded) as he walked among them, seemed to fortify the nagging urgency of marriage to fulfil the popular romantic ideal. Yet for years he picked and chose his way through a chain of girlfriends without even giving the appearance of the earnest prospective bridegroom – an attitude which at one time suggested the unthinkable; that he would remain a bachelor for want of a woman good enough in his responsible eyes to

Although rumour had it that Diana was not fond of polo, she dispelled the myth by accompanying Prince Charles to matches at Windsor whenever possible. Towards the end of her pregnancy doctors were on hand in case of emergency.

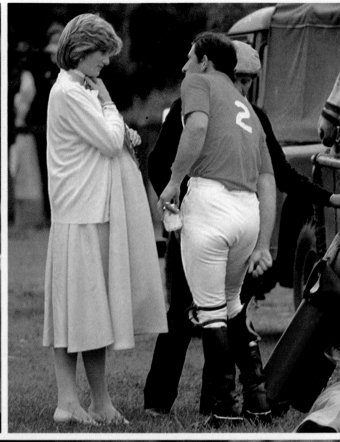

Diana wore her condition with a natural pride. Unlike so many expectant royal mothers who have avoided public appearances when pregnancy became obvious, the Princess continued to be seen until the very last days. These pages: At Windsor, just five days before the birth of Prince William.

become Queen to the Crown of over a thousand years. His accomplishment of the long transition from the shy adolescent to the mature, intelligent and questing adult seemed to have made him too demanding in the choice of a suitable wife possessing evidence of the same strength of character.

Deceptively vulnerable as she appeared to be on that late February day when her engagement was announced to the world, Diana enjoyed a large measure of that very quality. Her past had borne fruit. The history of her uneasy childhood – her parents' separation, with its sequel of prolonged, bitter and very public divorce proceedings, the disintegration of a stable home life, her mediocre educational progress culminating in an unsatisfactory interlude at finishing school – is now well known, but it has become increasingly apparent in the last year that, in coping with those

Although leisure time throughout 1982 was at a premium for the Prince of Wales, he did manage to play polo on a number of occasions during the busy summer months. Despite his inability to participate in the sport on anything but an irregular basis, he is acknowledged as being an accomplished player and captained his side to a fine win in the Mountbatten Cup. With Ascot relatively near to Windsor, matches are generally arranged for afternoons of each of the four days of racing, and it was to Smith's Lawn that Princess Diana repaired after her day at the racecourse.

successive domestic perplexities, she has developed a capacity for facing almost any of the novel eventualities which her new role

introduced into her life. Under the sympathetic eye of the Queen Mother, with whom she stayed between her engagement and her marriage, and coached by Lady Susan Hussey, the Queen's senior Lady in Waiting, she fairly slipped into the hectic daily round which characterised her early royal duties, and merged without undue difficulty into the pattern of high ceremonial which will punctuate

her official diary for the rest of her life.

The Queen could have paid no higher compliment to her new daughter-in-law, nor given a more positive sign of confidence in her, than to have found a place for her in the 1981 Royal Christmas Broadcast. The televised message included film of an informal ceremony in the grounds of Buckingham Palace in which physically handicapped people received keys to

The obviously proud new parents emerged from St Mary's hospital, less than 24 hours after the baby's birth, to the rapturous cheers of a crowd that had gathered there as soon as news of the Princess' admittance had become known.

Lord Snowdon's charming studies of the happy family were the first official pictures to be published showing the new prince, who obliged his great uncle by assuming expressions of interest. Although second in line to the throne after Prince Charles, the infant Prince will no doubt continue to upstage his father for some time to come. If he inherits the qualities of both parents, then he is assured of the hearts of his future subjects.

specially designed vehicles awarded to them during the Year of the Disabled. Diana was one of the four members of the Royal Family, along with the Queen, Prince Philip and Prince Charles, to distribute the keys and speak with the recipients. In the comparatively short history of televised Christmas broadcasts, this was a notable 'first.' The seven months between the announcement that Diana was expecting her baby and the date of Prince William's birth were not particularly busy ones as far as her official diary was concerned and, despite the massive publicity given to each public appearance, her 'performance' under the constant pressure of a full year's

Prince William's official debut – the christening at Buckingham Palace – coincided with another important occasion, the 82nd birthday of the Queen Mother. Diana's finger ensured that her baby's behaviour remained suitably regal!

programme of engagements could only be guessed at. At present she faces that daunting test as her autumn and winter schedule gets underway. In particular she can look forward – though perhaps with some trepidation – to a six-week tour of Australia and New Zealand in February and March 1983 and to an official visit to Canada later that year. They will be hectic times, of which she will have no comparable previous experience. Only the three-day tour of Wales in October 1981, with its ten and twelve-hour schedules, can give her the remotest hint of the hard slog and long days ahead. The

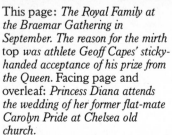

This page: *The Royal Family at the Braemar Gathering in September. The reason for the mirth top was athlete Geoff Capes' sticky-handed acceptance of his prize from the Queen.* Facing page and overleaf: *Princess Diana attends the wedding of her former flat-mate Carolyn Pride at Chelsea old church.*

Australians, already favoured by three official visits by the Queen and Prince Philip in as many years, are now looking forward to being the first of the old dominions to greet a Princess of Wales to their shores, and it will be a difficult job to keep the demands on her time down to a practicable and acceptable level. If the already rife speculation materialises, and Prince William goes with her, the Diana cult will surely surpass all expectations. The Queen, however, is aware from her long experience of steering the Monarchy between the Scylla of remoteness and the Charybdis of over-familiarity, that nothing exceeds like excess. As head of the family, and a force much to be reckoned with, she will allow Diana to take her son away only on conditions which avoid the worst extremes of publicity.

We live in an age when almost everything seems possible, and when consequently almost everything is taken for granted. The Monarchy has been with us for so long that logically it should have exhausted its appeal decades or even centuries ago. But to say so ignores the value of personal commitment and of the occasional timely touch of fresh blood. Diana has, in less than two years, provided that – and more. Which is why we can be confident about the institution in which she will one day be Queen Consort – about its future and its gentle, popular and beneficial influence on the society of the twenty-first century.

First English Edition published by Colour Library International Ltd.
© 1982 Illustrations and Text: Colour Library International Ltd.
    99 Park Avenue, New York, N.Y. 10016, U.S.A.
This edition published by Greenwich House, a division of Arlington
House, Inc., distributed by Crown Publishers, Inc.
h g f e d c b a
Colour separations by FER-CROM, Barcelona, Spain
Display and text filmsetting by ACESETTERS LTD., Richmond, Surrey, England.
Printed and bound in Barcelona, Spain by RIEUSSET and EUROBINDER
All rights reserved
ISBN 0-517-402718

D L.B.: 36301-82